SCHOLASTIC

Circle-Time Poetry
Around the Year

by Jodi Simpson

NEW YORK • TORONTO • LONDON • AUCKLAND • SYDNEY **Teaching** Resources
MEXICO CITY • NEW DELHI • HONG KONG • BUENOS AIRES

❀ **To my sisters.** ❀
Your love and support are poetry to my heart.

Cover art by Brenda Sexton
Cover design by Maria Lilja
Interior design by Sydney Wright
Interior art by Bari Weissman

ISBN: 0-439-52975-1
Copyright © 2005 by Jodi Simpson
Published by Scholastic Inc.
All rights reserved.
Printed in the U.S.A.

1 2 3 4 5 6 7 8 9 10   40   13 12 11 10 09 08 07 06 05

Contents

Introduction

Reading and writing and creating with children . . . Wow! Aren't we lucky as teachers to work alongside our students and watch them experiment with sounds, words, ideas, and images! I love reading aloud to children and seeing them delight in the sound of words. They love to say words over and over, enjoying the way the words feel on their tongues. They love silly words, strange-sounding words, big words, little words, and self-created words. They love to probe into the meanings of words, explore new ideas, and make connections with their own experiences.

This curiosity about words extends to printed language, too. Children notice the interesting lines and curves that form different letters. They are attracted to the squiggly shape of a question mark or the emphatic posture of an exclamation point. Seeing students' excitement about language gets me excited as well. It is this excitement that inspires me to spend quality time sharing the magic of spoken and written words with children every day of the school year.

I've always found that exploring poetry is a wonderful way to make the most of young children's fascination with language. Children are naturally drawn to poetry—its wordplay and musical sounds; its rhythm and rhyme and repetition. The language in poetry speaks to their hearts as well as their minds. It stirs up vivid pictures and memories that they just can't wait to share.

Connections to the Standards

The activities in this book are designed to support you in meeting the language arts standards recommended for children in early childhood. See page 7, for more.

As a teacher, I would find myself looking through scores of books trying to locate the perfect poems to read with my class. It was hard to find poems that met my instructional needs and that were just right for young children. Sometimes the poems were too long or the vocabulary was too advanced. So I began to write my own poems to share with my students. Now I'd like to share these poems with you and your students. I hope you will find them both useful and fun as your class embarks on its own wondrous adventures with words.

What's Inside

This book includes 20 seasonally-themed poems to spark children's imaginations and to use as springboards for listening, speaking, reading, and writing activities. I like to introduce the poems to children during circle time. We continue to work with a poem over the course of a week—or even several weeks—so that children can interact with the text repeatedly. As we read a poem again and again, children become more familiar with the words and more confident in reciting the lines. They begin to predict which word comes next and can focus better on the details, listening for specific sounds and searching for specific letters. During the period we are working with a poem, I like to include plenty of opportunities for children to respond to it orally, in writing, and through art. To help you make the most of each poem in this book, I've organized the accompanying lessons into the following sections:

Introducing the Poem

Here you'll find ideas for presenting the poem to your class. I always write the poems in large print on a sheet of chart paper. (You could also photocopy the poem pages onto an overhead.) This allows children to see clearly the words, spaces, and punctuation, and to follow along as you read. Children can come up to the chart paper and easily point out letters and words. To spark students' curiosity about the poem, I usually draw an interesting shape around it. For example, if the poem is about apples, I'll draw the outline of an apple around the words.

Use a pointer to track the print as you read the poem aloud several times. Children can chime in when they begin to feel comfortable with the words. You may want to invite children to act out the poem, do a finger play, or clap along to the rhythm as you read. I've included some read-aloud suggestions for each poem. (For tips on using the reproducible versions of the poems, see page 7.)

Talking About the Poem

In this section, you'll find discussion starters to get students thinking and talking about the poem. I want children to tap into their prior knowledge about a subject and to make connections to their own lives. I also ask specific questions about the content of the poem to check students' comprehension and ask imaginative questions to stimulate their creative thinking.

You'll also find suggestions for getting students to interact with the text. You may wish to ask children to listen for repeated sounds or rhyming words. You can invite them to come up and point to capital letters or letters that appear in their own names. You may want to count all the *w*'s or *t*'s in a poem, underline action words or color words, search for *-ing* endings, point out similar spelling patterns, and so on. If you laminate the chart paper, you can use wipe-off markers to underline or circle specific letters or words. Otherwise, you can simply place self-sticking notes under the letters or words that you wish to highlight.

Working With Words

This section includes ideas for simple games and activities to give students additional practice with some of the sounds, letters, and words featured in the poems. For example, if my students and I read a poem with several words from the -*ay* word family, I'll introduce a rhyming game to extend the learning. We may toss a ball around a circle as students come up with -*ay* rhyming words. Or we may play an improvised game of "Duck, Duck, Goose," substituting -*ay* rhyming words for the word "duck" and non-rhyming words for the word "goose."

In addition to rhyming games, this section includes ideas for word sorts, matching games, and other activities that allow children to explore a wide range of sounds, letters, and words. I've tried to include a variety of ideas from which you can choose and adapt according to your instructional needs and students' levels of ability.

Shared Writing

I like to use the poems as springboards to group writing activities. Together, my students and I create simple list poems, word webs, and charts. Or we may complete sentence frames or write collaborative letters. I want children to connect with the content of a poem by sharing their own experiences, observations, and knowledge about a topic. As students dictate, I write their ideas on the chalkboard or chart paper, sounding out each letter. This is a chance to model the writing process—to show children that letters represent sounds, that words represent ideas, and that writing proceeds from top to bottom and left to right. But most important, it's a chance to give form to children's own words and thoughts. My students get a kick out of watching me write what they are saying. It's powerful to "see" language on paper, especially for young children.

Extending the Poem

I also like to give students a chance to connect with a poem through art. It's another way for them to experience the poem's words and themes. Art activities also lend our poetry lessons a hands-on quality that really engages young children.

In this section, you'll find suggestions for projects in which children respond to the poem using a variety of art media and techniques, including painting, printmaking, and collage. I like to display children's artwork alongside a copy of the poem. Sometimes children write the poem directly onto their finished artwork. It is interesting and informative to see the ways different children interpret and represent the poems. The children are so proud to display their work. They giggle at each other's artistic creations and proudly point out their own. Reciting the now-familiar words of the poems in their artwork displays builds their confidence and helps children see themselves as readers. I also enjoy sending these poetic creations home with children to share with their families.

Literature Links

This section provides reading suggestions that tie in nicely with a poetry selection. Use the books to capitalize on students' interest in a theme presented in a poem or to take a topic of study further.

Reproducible Poems

Each lesson includes a reproducible copy of the poem. Students enjoy having their own copies of the poems so they can color the illustrations and take a closer look at the words. You may want to provide children with copies of the poems *after* you've introduced the poem to the entire class during read-aloud time. As you model reading for children and point out various phonological elements, you'll want all eyes focused on what you are doing. Later, when you reread the poem and continue exploring the poem's sounds, letters, and words, you can provide children with individual copies. That way students can circle and underline the letters and words on the handouts that you highlight on chart paper.

I also make a habit of sending home copies of the poems with students. It's nice for caregivers to learn the poems along with children. They can then recite the poems with children while driving in the car, setting the table, or washing children's hair in the bathtub.

Reproducible Pattern Pages

Reproducible pattern pages accompany a number of the lessons. You can incorporate these patterns into the lessons in different ways. There are patterns for creating puppets to use as props in poetry read-alouds, for making word walls, and for assembling seasonally-themed shape books, among other activities. Suggestions and directions for using the patterns are included in the poetry lesson plans.

Connections to the Early Childhood Standards: Language Arts

The activities in this book are designed to support you in meeting the following recommendations and goals for early reading and writing put forth in a joint position statement by the International Reading Association (IRA) and the National Association for the Education of Young Children (NAEYC). These goals describe a continuum for children's development in grades PreK-1:

- understands that print carries a message
- recognizes left-to-right and top-to-bottom orientation and basic concepts of print
- engages in and talks about reading and writing experiences
- uses descriptive language to explain and explore
- recognizes letters, letter-sound matches, and matches spoken words with written ones
- shows familiarity with rhyming and beginning sounds
- builds a sight word vocabulary

Source: *Learning to Read and Write: Developmentally Appropriate Practices for Young Children* © 1998 by The National Association for the Education of Young Children.

Mmm ... Apple Pie!

Apples, apples! Crispy, crunchy,
juicy, sweet, mighty munchy!
Climbing, climbing up so high,
to pick some apples for a pie.
Twist them, turn them, pick them quick.
Pulling hard will do the trick.
Our basket's full, so off we go
to slice the apples, roll the dough.
Add some sugar, spices too
a pinch of cinnamon, that will do.
Bake it, bake it, till it's done.
Apple pie! Yum, yum, yum!

Circle-Time Poetry: Around the Year Scholastic Teaching Resources

Mmm . . . Apple Pie!

Introducing the Poem

- Write the poem on chart paper. Draw a large outline of an apple or apple pie around the words.

- For a whimsical touch, wear a chef's hat and use a wooden spoon to track the words as you read the poem aloud.

- Invite children to pantomime all the different actions mentioned in the poem, such as biting into an apple, climbing a ladder, picking the apples, rolling the dough, and so on. For the last line, children can lick their lips and rub their bellies.

Talking About the Poem

- Have students ever gone apple picking? Ask them to describe their experiences. What other foods are made from apples? What are students' favorite apple treats?

- Draw students' attention to alliterative phrases such as *crispy*, *crunchy*, and *mighty munchy*. What sounds do students hear repeated? What letters make these sounds?

- Ask students to help you find all the action words in the poem. Circle them on the chart paper.

Working With Words

Rhyming Word Apple Toss: Play a simple game that focuses on some of the rhyming words in the poem. Toss a small apple to one student. Ask, "Can you tell me a word that rhymes with *pie*?" After the student provides a rhyming word, have him or her throw the apple back to you. Continue tossing the apple around the circle, challenging students to come up with all the rhymes they can for the word *pie*. When you've exhausted that word, choose another from the poem and continue the game.

Shared Writing

Apple Pie List Poem: Together, write a class list poem about this tasty autumn treat. Write the words *Apple Pie* at the top of a sheet of chart paper. Ask children to brainstorm words that describe what apple pie looks, smells, and tastes like. List their ideas. End the poem with the words *Apple Pie*.

Apple Pie
golden
warm
cinnamon
sweet
juicy
Apple Pie

Literature Links

These excellent books celebrate autumn and apples:

The Apple Pie Tree by Zoe Hall (Scholastic, 1996)

Autumn Is for Apples by Michelle Knudsen (Random House, 2001)

Extending the Poem

Apple Pie Flap Book

Follow these directions to help students prepare make-believe apple pies that smell as delicious as the real thing!

Materials

❀ apple pie patterns pages (11–12)

❀ scissors

❀ crayons

❀ glue sticks

❀ cinnamon

❀ glitter (tan, brown, white, or silver)

❶ Make one double-sided photocopy of the apple pie pattern for each child. The crust should be on one side of the paper, the writing activity on the other. Have children cut out the pattern along the outer dotted lines.

❷ Tell students to position the pattern so that the writing activity is faceup on their desk. Next have them fold down the top part of the pattern to make a flap. The scalloped edges of the pie should line up with the pie pan, as shown.

❸ Have students color the pie, and apply a small amount of glue to the top crust. They can lightly sprinkle cinnamon and glitter onto the crust to give the pie a fresh-from-the-oven aroma and a sparkly sugared topping.

❹ Tell children to lift the flap and write a list of words describing what apple pie looks, smells, and tastes like. Display your list poem from the shared writing activity so that students can use it as a mini word bank.

Note: If you can't make double-sided copies, photocopy each page separately. Have students cut out the two patterns. Then have them follow the directions in step 2, above. To complete the pie, direct them to glue the piecrust top (from page 11) to the flap so that the piecrust is sitting on the pie pan.

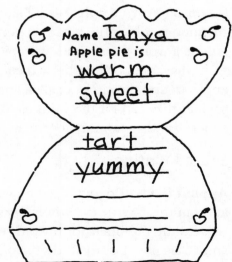

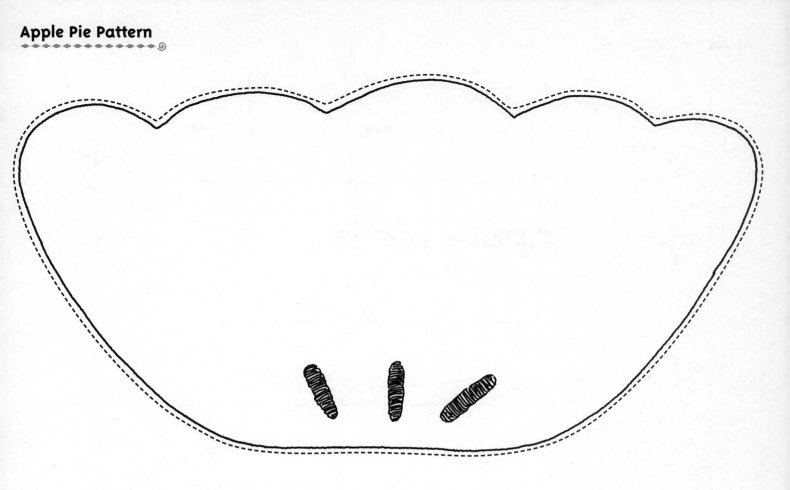

Name _____

Apple pie is

_____

_____

_____

_____

_____

Autumn Leaves

Autumn leaves, they flutter
as they fall down to the ground.
They whirl, they twirl, they dance,
but they don't make a sound.
Quiet, oh-so-quiet,
they whisper on their way,
landing in a pile
in which we all can play.

Autumn Leaves

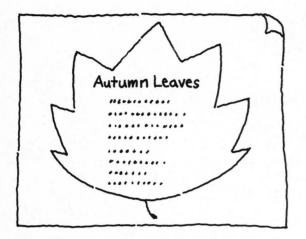

Introducing the Poem

🌀 Write the poem on chart paper. Draw the outline of a leaf around the words.

🌀 Provide each child with a real leaf. Before reading the poem aloud, tell children to toss their leaves in the air and watch them flutter to the ground. Ask children to think of words that describe the way the leaves move.

🌀 After you have read the poem aloud a few times, invite students to move like leaves. Let them pretend to flutter through the air as you read the poem again.

Talking About the Poem

✿ Encourage children to think about how quietly leaves fall. What other things can they think of that are "quiet as a whisper"? Offer some ideas to spur their thinking (for example, a flower growing, a mouse sleeping, eyes blinking, a feather floating).

✿ Point out the word *whisper*. What letter does this word begin with? Challenge children to find three other words in the poem that begin with *w*.

✿ Circle the word *ground*. Can children find the word that rhymes with it? Circle the word *way* and challenge them to find the word that rhymes with this word, too. Point out the similar spelling patterns in each pair of rhymes.

Working With Words

Word Family Circle Game: On chart paper, write a list of words from the *-ay* word family (for example, *lay, say, pay, bay, may, gray, play, tray, clay*). Use these words to play a modified game of "Duck, Duck, Goose." Move around the circle of children, saying an *-ay* word as you tap each person. Then randomly introduce a nonrhyming word (for example, *way, play, day, say, house*). When you say the nonrhyming word, the child you tapped gives chase. Repeat the game, with students taking turns reciting the rhymes.

Shared Writing

Autumn Leaves Word Tree: Ask students to brainstorm words that describe what autumn leaves look like and the way they move. List their ideas on a sheet of chart paper. Make multiple copies of the leaf patterns on page 16 and cut them out. Provide each child with a leaf shape to color. Then have each

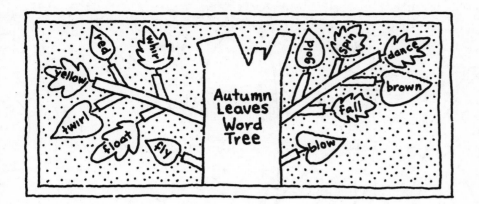

child copy a word from the list onto a leaf. Use brown construction paper to make a tree trunk and branches. Attach the tree pattern to a bulletin board, then add the leaves to complete your word tree.

Extending the Poem

Leaf Rubbing Quilt

Children make leaf rubbings to get a closer look at these bright beacons of fall.

Materials

✿ leaves (assorted shapes, colors, and sizes)

✿ crayons (in various autumn colors, with paper wrappers removed)

✿ scrap paper

✿ 8-inch squares of thin white paper

✿ 10-inch squares of colored paper (red, orange, and yellow)

✿ glue

✿ tape

❶ Have children put a piece of scrap paper on their desk, place a leaf on top of it, and then cover the leaf with a white paper square.

❷ Demonstrate how to hold a crayon sideways and rub it over the paper square until the leaf's shape and pattern appears. Show children how they can rub additional crayons, in different colors, over the leaf to make the rubbing more vibrant.

❸ Invite children to make their rubbing. Then have them glue it onto a square of colored paper.

❹ Arrange the squares in a pattern and tape them together to make a quilt. Display the quilt in a prominent place, and invite children to compare the different shapes and patterns on their leaf rubbings.

✶ ◌ Literature Links ◌ ✶

Here are several books that invite young readers to further explore and delight in the seasonal changes that fall brings.

Autumn Leaves by Ken Robbins (Scholastic, 1998)

Fresh Fall Leaves by Betsy Franco (Scholastic, 1994)

How Do You Know It's Fall? by Allan Fowler (Children's Press, 1992)

It's Fall by Linda Glaser (Millbrook Press, 2001)

Leaf Patterns

Pumpkin Nights

Pumpkins on the windowsills
shining out so bright.
Gleaming, glowing jack-o'-lanterns
lighting up the night.
Watching us with winking eyes
as we walk down the street.
Flashing us their zigzag grins
as we call "trick-or-treat!"
Pumpkins on the windowsills
shining out so bright.
Gleaming, glowing jack-o'-lanterns
lighting up the night.

Pumpkin Nights

Introducing the Poem

◎ Write the poem on chart paper. Draw the outline of a pumpkin around the words.

◎ Children may enjoy using the following hand gestures to highlight the different images within the poem as you read it aloud:

Lines 1-2: Spread hands open around face in a circular motion to suggest the pumpkins' shining faces.

Lines 3-4: Extend arms over head in a circular motion to suggest the pumpkins lighting up the night.

Lines 5-6: Point to eyes and wink.

Lines 7-8: Point to mouth, then trace a zigzag shape in the air.

Lines 9-12: Repeat actions for first four lines.

Talking About the Poem

✿ Ask children to use their imaginations to think of reasons the jack-o'-lanterns might be grinning. Are they happy it's Halloween? Do they like the children's costumes?

✿ Draw students' attention to alliterative phrases such as *gleaming, glowing* and *watching us with winking eyes*. What sounds do they hear repeated?

✿ Challenge children to find and underline all the words that contain the phonogram *-ight*.

Working With Words

Word Family Pumpkin Toss: On chart paper, write the following list of words from the *-ight* word family: *bright, light, night, fight, might, right, sight, tight, flight, fright*. Then lead children in a sound blending activity. Begin by making the initial consonant sound for one of the words on your list, for example /l/. Pause briefly before saying *-ight*. Toss a miniature pumpkin to a student and ask him or her to blend the sounds together to say the word (in this instance, *light*). Then have that student toss the pumpkin back to you. Repeat the activity, tossing the pumpkin around the circle until you've segmented and blended all the words on your list.

Shared Writing

Pumpkin Expression Sentences: Write the following frame on the chalkboard:

Pumpkins can be _____.

Draw a picture of a grinning pumpkin. Ask children to finish the sentence by providing a word that describes the pumpkin's expression (for example, *happy*). Change the pumpkin's expression several times and each time ask students to substitute other words in the place of *happy*. Then provide each child with a copy of the pumpkin pattern on page 20. Have children cut out the pumpkin. Then have them complete the sentence frame on the front of the pumpkin and draw a matching expression on the back. Children can then color the pumpkin and fill in their name. Punch holes in the tops of the pumpkins and bind them together to make a class shape-book.

Extending the Poem

Pumpkin Magic

Students will enjoy a bit of Halloween "magic" as they make their own brightly shining pumpkins using coffee filters and tinted water.

Materials

- water
- paper cups
- food coloring (red and yellow)
- old newspapers
- round coffee filters
- eyedroppers
- precut green paper rectangles (about 1/2 by 3 inches)
- precut black paper triangles (about 1 1/2 inches tall)
- glue

1. Put about 1/4 cup of water into each of a number of paper cups. Add 8 to 10 drops of red food coloring to half of the cups, and 8 to 10 drops of yellow food coloring to the other half. Set out enough cups of each color for your class to share.

2. Spread out newspapers and provide each child with two coffee filters stacked together and flattened. (Using two filters provides added durability.)

3. Have children use an eyedropper to squeeze drops of the red and yellow water onto the filters. Wow! Students will be fascinated as they watch the colors "magically" mix together to make orange.

4. After the filters dry, students can glue on a green rectangle "stem," and black triangles for eyes, a nose, and a toothy grin.

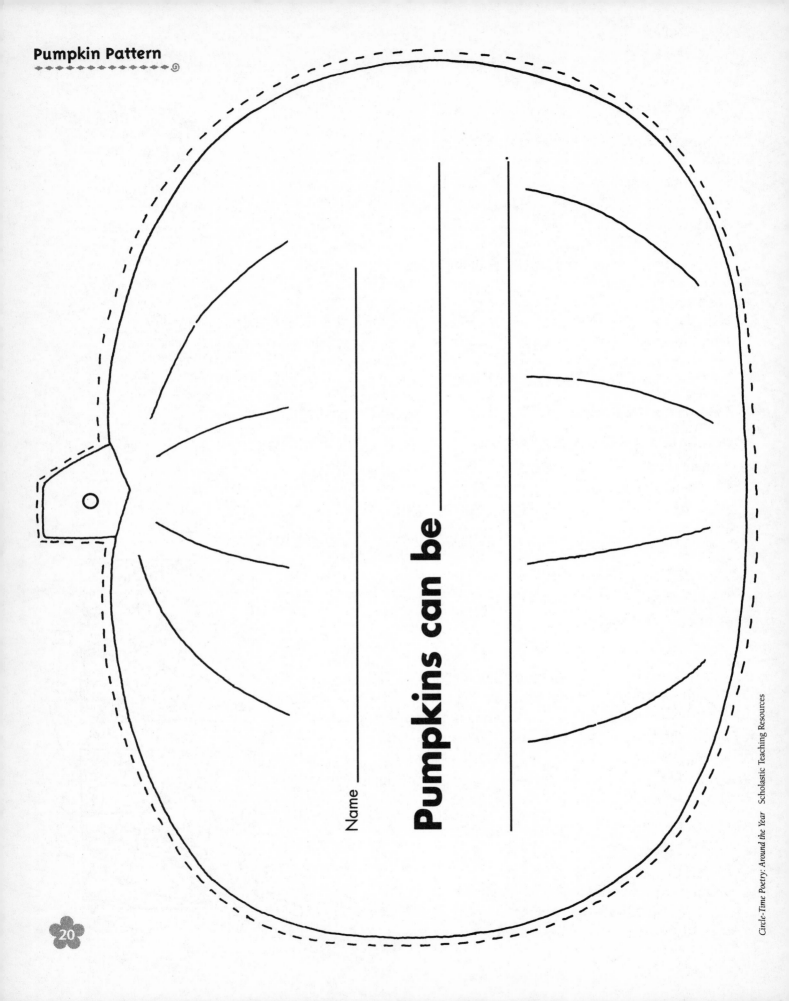

Name

Pumpkins can be

Circle-Time Poetry: Around the Year Scholastic Teaching Resources

Thanks For ...

Thank you for so many things.
For the songs of birds and butterfly wings,
for the sun that warms us with its light,
for stars that twinkle in the night,
for eyes that see and ears that hear,
for family and friends so dear,
for grass below and sky above
for a head to dream and heart to love.

Thanks For . . .

Introducing the Poem

◎ Write the poem on chart paper. Draw the outline of a turkey around the words.

◎ Invite children to read the poem in a call-and-response manner, repeating each line after you say it aloud.

◎ Reread the poem but this time invite children to act out different lines. For example, children might flap their arms gently to be *butterfly wings*, reach up and wiggle their fingers for the phrase *stars that twinkle in the night*, and point to their eyes and ears when you read the line *for eyes that see and ears that hear*.

Talking About the Poem

✿ Begin a discussion with children about all the things they are thankful for in their own lives. Encourage them to think of their families, friends, pets, things in nature, and special places.

✿ Point out that the word *Thanksgiving* begins with *th*. Review how to pronounce this digraph. Ask children to count how many words in the poem begin with *th*. Do they know any other words that begin with the sound /th/?

Working With Words

Naming Words Song: Cut out pictures from magazines that depict some of the items mentioned in the poem (for example, *birds, butterfly, stars, sun, eyes, ears, grass, head,* and *heart*). Glue each picture onto an unlined index card. On the back of each card write the word that corresponds to the picture. Place the cards word side up in the middle of the circle of students. Walk around in a circle holding hands as you sing these words to the tune of "The Farmer in the Dell":

We're thankful for the birds. We're thankful for the birds.
High-ho, the derry-o. We're thankful for the birds.

Call out the name of a student and have him or her go to the center of the circle to find the card with the word *birds*. The child can check the picture on the other side to make sure he or she has chosen the correct card. Repeat the game, substituting other words for *birds*, until all of the cards have been collected.

Shared Writing

We Are Thankful Chart: Prepare a simple three-column chart with the headings *At Home*, *At School*, and *In Nature*. Ask students to come up with things they are thankful for in each of these categories. List their ideas under the appropriate heading.

At Home	At School	In Nature
pets	books	trees
family	friends	grass
clothes	crayons	flowers
toys	games	birds

Extending the Poem

Thanks For . . . Turkeys

Students will enjoy making these whimsical turkeys, which they can use to showcase the things they're thankful for.

Materials

❀ turkey pattern (page 24)

❀ 9- by 12-inch pieces of brown construction paper

❀ 1- by 9-inch strips of construction paper
(various bright colors; 5 per child)

❀ scraps of yellow and red construction paper

❀ scissors

❀ glue

❀ black markers

❶ Photocopy the turkey pattern onto brown construction paper and distribute. Have each child cut out the pattern.

❷ Show students how to create simple beaks, feet, and wattles from scraps of yellow and red construction paper. Have children glue these in place on their turkey's body. Then have them use a marker to add eyes.

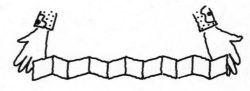

❸ Demonstrate how to fold the colored paper strips accordion style to create the turkey's feathers. Then have children glue the five feathers onto their turkey's body.

❹ Have children fill in their names on their turkey and help them list things they are thankful for on the lines provided.

Literature Links

These books will prompt students to reflect on the people and things that enrich their lives as they take a look at what inspires gratitude in others:

Feeling Thankful by Shelley Rotners and Sheila M. Kelly (Millbrook Press, 2000)

Giving Thanks: A Native American Good Morning Message by Jake Swamp (Lee & Low, 1997)

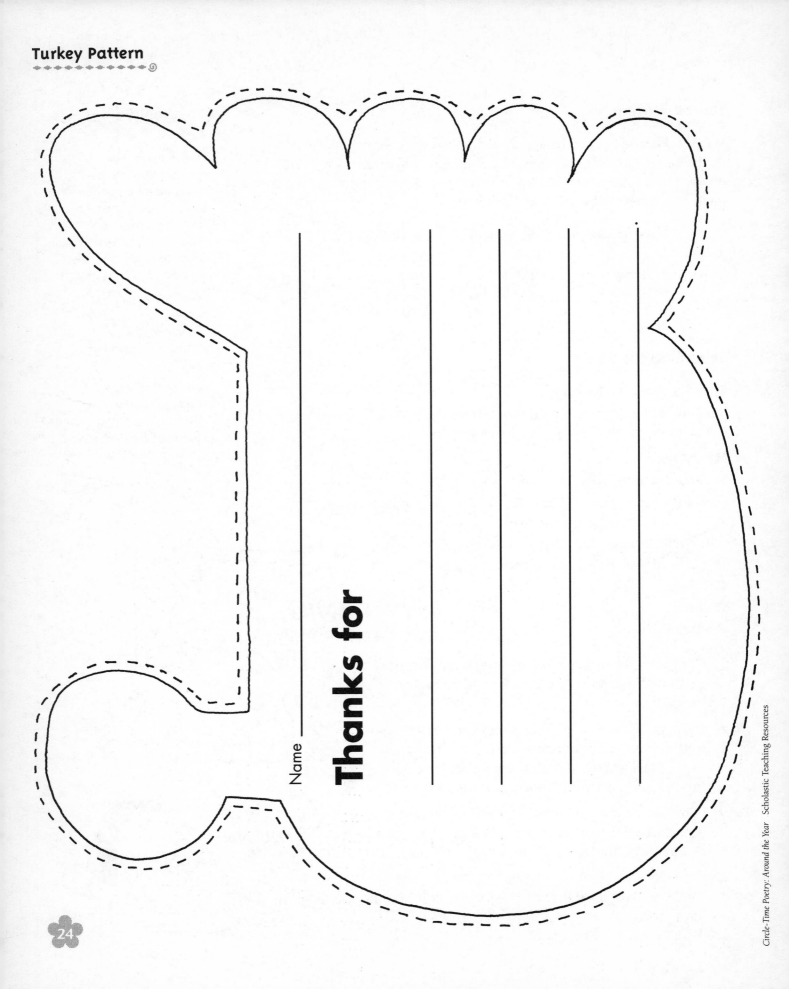

Name _____

Thanks for

Empty Branches

Empty branches
reach for the sky.
They feel the chill.
I hear them cry,
"Come back birds
and take your rest.
Use our arms
to cradle your nest.
We'll wait for you
with arms stretched high,
ready to catch you
from spring's blue sky."

Circle-Time Poetry: Around the Year   Scholastic Teaching Resources

Empty Branches

Empty Branches

Introducing the Poem

🌀 Write the poem on the lower part of a sheet of chart paper. Draw the outline of a tree trunk around the words. Show bare, empty branches extending up over the poem.

🌀 Invite children to stand up and imagine that they are trees. Have them reach their arms up high. Make a soft whistling sound and ask students to pretend their "branches" (arms) are swaying in the wind. Tell students to stand very still and quietly as you read the poem aloud. Ask them to pretend that they are trees in the fall waiting patiently for birds to return in the spring and build nests in their branches.

Talking About the Poem

❁ If you live in an area that doesn't experience the autumnal changes described in the poem, you may want to explain to students that, in many regions of the country, fall is when some trees lose their leaves. Can students think of other changes that happen in the fall? Why do some birds fly away when fall arrives?

❁ Ask students why the trees in the poem might want to have birds living among their branches. Encourage children to use their imaginations. Do the trees like to listen to the birds sing? Do they like to watch the baby birds grow?

❁ Use sticky notes to cover the words *cry* in line 4, *nest* in line 8, and *sky* in line 12. Reread the poem and ask children to try to guess the missing words.

Working With Words

Rhyming Word Leaves: Generate a list of rhyming words for *sky* and *nest*. Write each word on a leaf pattern (use the patterns on page 16). Have children help you color and cut out the leaves. Toss the leaves in the air so that they land in the center of the circle of students. Let children take turns picking up the leaves one by one and sorting them into two separate piles of rhyming words.

Shared Writing

Autumn Trees List Poem: Write the words *Autumn Trees* at the top of a sheet of chart paper. Ask students to think of words that describe what the trees look like and what feelings come to mind. List their ideas. At the bottom of the list, write the words *Autumn Trees* again to conclude the poem.

Extending the Poem

Collaborative Autumn Mural

In this hands-on project, children make a collaborative mural that illustrates the seasonal changes that occur in autumn.

Materials

❀ 6-foot piece of light-blue bulletin board paper
❀ washable paints (brown, dark blue, red, orange, yellow)
❀ paintbrushes
❀ black marker

Autumn Trees
tall
gray
empty
bare
lonely
waiting
Autumn Trees

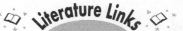
Literature Links

These books offer fanciful and fascinating looks, respectively, at a tree's changing appearance:

Fall Is Not Easy by Marty Kelley (Zino Press, 1998)

Red Leaf, Yellow Leaf by Lois Ehlert, (Harcourt, 1991)

❶ Draw a simple outline of a tree with several bare branches on the center of the bulletin board paper. Invite children to help you paint the trunk and branches brown.

❷ Use a brush to paint the hands of four or five students blue. Be sure to cover the palms and fingers of both hands.

❸ Show children how to make bird-shaped handprints on the top part of the bulletin board paper. Direct students to align their thumbs to form the body of the bird. Then have them slightly angle their fingers so that they resemble wings, as shown, right. Next have students position the "birds" on the paper to look like they are flying away from the tree.

❹ Paint the hands of the remaining students red, orange, and yellow. Direct these children to make handprints with their hands closed tightly, along the bottom of the blue paper to represent the tree's fallen leaves.

❺ Write the poem next to the tree to complete your mural.

Snow Angels

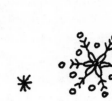

Making angels in the snow,
stretching out as we lie down.
Sweeping arms and sweeping legs,
making wings and gowns.
Making angels in the snow,
rising carefully as can be.
Leaving magic on the ground,
angel magic for all to see.

Snow Angels

Introducing the Poem

◉ Write the poem on chart paper. Draw the outline of an angel around the words.

◉ Have children stand up, leaving plenty of space between one another. As you read the poem aloud, children can pretend they are making snow angel wings with their arms, gently moving them up and down in rhythm to the words.

Talking About the Poem

✿ Have students ever made snow angels? Ask them to describe the process, step by step. If you live in an area that doesn't get snow, share books with students that include pictures of snowy scenes and snow angels. (See Literature Links, page 30.)

✿ Place sticky notes under the following words in the poem: *making, stretching, sweeping, rising,* and *leaving.* Ask children what all these words have in common. Invite volunteers to underline the *-ing* endings.

Working With Words

Word Family Snowball Toss: On a sheet of chart paper, write a list of rhyming words from the *-ow* word family (for example, *snow, glow, throw, bow, low, show, flow, grow, know, row*). Then lead children in a sound blending activity. Begin by making the initial consonant sound for the word snow — /sn/ — as you toss a Styrofoam "snowball" to a student. Have the student say "ow" as she or he catches the ball. The whole class then says, "snow." Continue tossing the snowball around the circle until you've segmented and blended all the *-ow* words on your list.

Shared Writing

Snow Play Word Web: Ask children to think about and describe all the different ways they play (or would like to play) in the snow. Create a word web to present their ideas.

29

Here are two beautiful books in which snow angels come magically to life:

The Snow Angel by Debby Boone (Harvest House, 1991)

Snow Angel by Jean Marzollo (Scholastic, 1995)

Extending the Poem

Sparkling Snow Angels

Follow these directions to create sparkling angels that look like they are made from freshly fallen snow.

Materials

❀ old newspapers   ❀ dark blue construction paper

❀ white finger paint   ❀ iridescent glitter

① Spread out newspapers on a table. Gather children around and demonstrate how to use the finger paint to make the angels (follow steps 2–8). Once you've completed your demonstration, have children paint their own angels.

② Squirt about two tablespoons of paint onto a sheet of blue paper. The paint should be slightly above the center of the page.

③ Press your hands together, aligning the palms and fingers. Place the sides of your hands onto the paper, so that the sides of your pinkies are pressed into the paint.

④ Spread the paint toward the edges of the paper by making sweeping, curving motions to create the angel's wings, as shown, right.

⑤ Squirt two more tablespoons of paint just below the wings. Align your hands in the same manner as before and press them into the paint again.

⑥ Spread the paint toward the edges of the paper by making sweeping, curving motions to create the angel's gown, as shown, right.

⑦ Squirt about a teaspoon of paint just above the wings. Swirl the paint to make the angel's head.

⑧ Sprinkle glitter over the paint and allow it to dry.

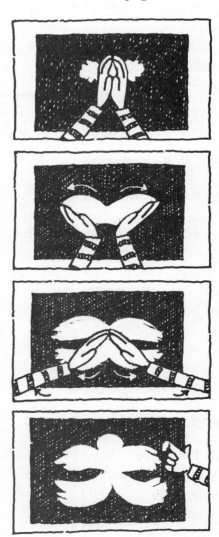

Candles
Glowing
Bright

Candles

Glowing bright

Peace

Love

Joy

Hope

Shining welcome

Candles

Circle-Time Poetry: Around the Year Scholastic Teaching Resources

Candles Glowing Bright

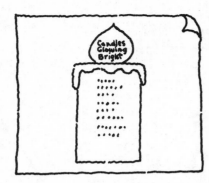

Introducing the Poem

🌀 Write the poem on chart paper. Draw the outline of a candle around the words. Draw a flame around the poem's title.

🌀 Bring in some scented candles. Invite children to feel the smooth texture of the wax and smell the different scents.

Talking About the Poem

✿ Begin a discussion with children about all the occasions at which they have seen candles. They may tell you about birthdays, Christmas, Hanukkah, Kwanzaa, or simply quiet moments at home. Ask them to think about and explain how the candles made them feel. Point out that people all over the world use candles as a sign of peace and to gain comfort.

✿ Because this is such a simple poem, it's easy to focus on the beginning sound of every word. Cover all the initial letters with sticky notes. As you read each word, emphasize its beginning sound. Pause and ask children to guess the missing letter.

Working With Words

Initial Consonant Match-Up: Continue working with initial sounds by playing a matching game. Write each word from the poem on a blank index card. Snip off the initial consonant or consonant cluster. Put the cards with the initial consonants in one pile and the remaining cards in a second pile. Mix up the cards in each pile. Then take a card from the initial consonants pile and place it to the left of a card from the other pile. Say each sound separately and then blend the sounds together. Do the cards belong together? Repeat the activity until students have matched all the cards.

Shared Writing

Make-a-Wish Candle Book: Have children ever made a wish before blowing out the candles on a birthday cake? Explain that this is one of the many traditions linked to candles. Write the following sentence frame several times on the chalkboard:

I wish that _____.

Invite volunteers to finish the sentence by sharing special wishes that they have for themselves, their loved ones, or the world. Write down what students dictate. Then provide each child with a copy of the candle pattern on page 34. (Photocopy the page onto heavyweight paper for added durability.) Help each child write his or her wish on the pattern. Then have children fill in their names and decorate their candles using crayons, markers, glitter, and so on. Cut out the patterns and then tape them together, side by side, to create an accordion-style class shape-book. Fold up the book and place it in the reading center or display it, unfolded, on a bulletin board.

Extending the Poem

Sponge Print Candles

Make your classroom glow with these bright sponge-print candle designs.

Materials

- ✿ rectangular kitchen sponges (about 10)
- ✿ scissors
- ✿ scrap paper
- ✿ old newspapers
- ✿ pie tins
- ✿ tempera paints (various colors)
- ✿ 12- by 18-inch sheets of white construction paper
- ✿ markers

Literature Links

These books highlight some of the different ways people use candles in holiday celebrations:

The Farolitos of Christmas by Rudolfo Anaya (Hyperion, 1995)

Light the Candle! Bang the Drum!: A Book of Holidays Around the World by Ann Morris (Dutton, 1997)

Light the Candles: A Hanukkah Lift-the-Flap Book by Joan Holub (Puffin, 2000)

Seven Candles for Kwanzaa by Andrea Davis Pinkney (Dial, 1993)

❶ Cut half of the sponges down the middle, lengthwise and crosswise to create simple candle shapes.

❷ Draw a flame shape on a piece of scrap paper. Cut out the flame shape. Use it as a template to draw two flame shapes on each of the remaining sponges. Cut out the flame shapes from the sponges.

❸ Spread out newspapers and pour different colors of paint into several pie tins. Be sure to include yellow among the colors.

❹ Show students how to dip a candle-shaped sponge into paint, wipe off any excess, and press onto paper to create a candle print. Repeat the process with a flame-shaped sponge. Let students practice making candle prints on scrap paper.

❺ Have each child copy the poem "Candles Glowing Bright" onto the center of a sheet of white construction paper.

❻ Students can then decorate the poem by surrounding it with candle-shaped sponge prints.

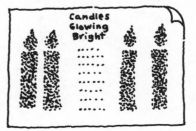

Candles Glowing Bright

I wish that

_____

_____

_____

_____

_____ .

Name _____

Circle-Time Poetry: Around the Year Scholastic Teaching Resources

New Year's Day

This is New Year's Day, they say.
Time to start out fresh, they say.
So this year I'll do my best
to make it better than the rest.
Sharing, helping, learning more
than I ever did before.
New adventures, friends to meet,
songs to sing, and books to read.
So much to see and do and know.
The New Year's here! Ready, set, go!

Circle-Time Poetry: Around the Year Scholastic Teaching Resources

New Year's Day

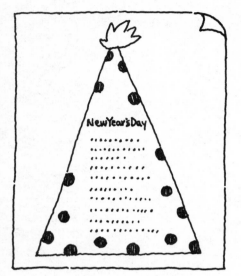

Introducing the Poem

- Write the poem on chart paper. Draw the outline of a party hat around the words.

- If you have party hats available, give one to each child to wear. (To make a simple party hat for each child, cut a slit into the center of a paper plate. Hold the plate on a child's head and overlap the cut parts until they fit like a hat. Staple closed. Invite children to decorate their hats using shapes cut from scrap paper, stickers, glitter, and more.)

- Provide each child with a small handful of confetti. Tell children to listen carefully as you read the poem aloud. When they hear you say *Ready, set, go!* in the last line, invite them to toss their confetti in the air and shout, "Happy New Year!"

Talking About the Poem

- Ask children to share their thoughts about why people get excited about the start of a new year. What new adventures would your students like to have in the year ahead? How can they do their best to make this year "better than the rest"?

- What words in the poem begin with the blend *fr*? (*fresh* and *friends*) Reread the poem and ask children to raise their hands every time they hear a word that begins with this blend. What other words can children think of that begin with the same sound?

- Can students find the two rhyming words in the first line of the poem? After they identify *day* and *say*, ask students what they notice about the last two letters in these words. Point out that you can turn *day* into *say* by replacing the *d* with an *s*.

Working With Words

Word Family Pocket Chart: Continue working with the *-ay* word family. On an index card, write the word *day*. Write the following initial consonants and consonant clusters on index cards that you have cut in half crosswise: *m, s, p, h, b, w, pl, gr*. Write these letters near the right edge of each card. Place the letter cards along the bottom of the pocket chart. Ask, "How can we change *day* to *may*?" Invite a volunteer to place the letter card over the *d*. Continue challenging students to form new words by substituting letters.

Shared Writing

A-New-Year-Ahead! Chart: Ask children to think about what they would like to see, do, and learn in the new year. Are there any people that they would like to meet, special places that they would like to visit, or activities that they would like to try? What would they like to learn in the year ahead? Create a three-column chart to show students' ideas.

See	Do	Learn
dinosaurs at the museum	go sledding	how to write
the ocean	go skating	how to count to 100
my cousins	get a dog	how to whistle

Extending the Poem

New Year Noisemakers

Give the new year a noisy welcome with these celebratory noisemakers!

Materials

❀ bathroom tissue tubes
❀ markers
❀ stickers
❀ hole punch
❀ 5 1/2-inch squares of waxed paper
❀ rubber bands

❶ Provide each child with a cardboard tube. Children can decorate the tubes using the markers and stickers.

❷ Use the hole punch to make a hole in one end of each child's tube, as shown.

❸ Help children use the rubber band to attach the waxed paper to the end of the tube that has the hole.

❹ Demonstrate how to blow into the open end of the tube. Tell children to try covering the hole with their fingers to create different sounds.

❺ Invite each child to tell the class something new that he or she would like to see, learn, or do in the new year. Have the rest of the class toot their noisemakers in response to cheer for their friends.

Literature Links

The first two books below follow a character through a year, highlighting a new adventure for each new month. The second two books focus on New Year's celebrations and traditions:

A Kitten's Year by Nancy Raines Day (HarperCollins, 1999)

A Time to Keep by Tasha Tudor (Simon & Schuster, 1996)

Happy New Year, Beni by Jane Breskin Zalben (Henry Holt, 1993)

Three Wishes by Lucille Clifton (Dell, 1993)

hole

Moonlight Painter

Jack Frost came to our house
in the middle of the night,
painting silver, icy pictures
by the glow of the moon's light.
His brush made glitter swirls,
pretty patterns, too.
His strokes of magic glisten
like a frosty winter dew.

Circle-Time Poetry: Around the Year Scholastic Teaching Resources

Moonlight Painter

Introducing the Poem

Write the poem on chart paper. Draw a crescent moon curving around the words. You may want to add facial features to suggest that the moon is watching over the wintry scene the poem describes.

Have children take turns pretending to be Jack Frost. Provide a ski cap for them to wear and a paintbrush to hold. As you read the poem aloud, "Jack Frost" can tiptoe in and pretend to paint swirls, zigzags, and other designs in the air.

Talking About the Poem

Have students ever seen frosty patterns on their windows when they wake up in the morning? What designs did they notice? How do they think the patterns got there?

How many words can children find in the poem that begin with the letter cluster *gl*? Invite volunteers to circle these words. How many words can they find that begin with *p*? Have students underline these words.

Working With Words

Rhyming Word Freeze: Provide each child with a paintbrush. Ask students to pretend that they are Jack Frost, and have them paint patterns in the air. Choose a word from the poem and slowly recite a list of rhymes for it (for example, *swirls, whirls, twirls, curls, girls*). Then introduce a nonrhyming word (for example, *dog*). When children hear you say a nonrhyming word, tell them to freeze immediately in place. Have them "unfreeze" and continue painting when they hear you begin a new list of rhyming words. Some other good words to use might be *Jack, night, glow, brush,* and *dew*.

Shared Writing

What-the-Moon-Sees Word Web: Ask children to pretend that there's a "man in the moon" watching everything that happens at night. Besides Jack Frost's make-believe magic, what else would the moon see? Encourage children to use their imaginations as they think about what people, animals, plants, and even buildings are doing at night. Create a word web to present their ideas.

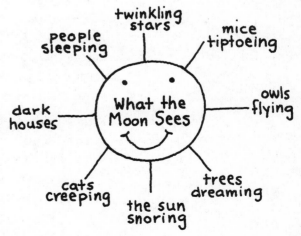

Literature Links

These imaginative stories capture the enchantment of winter weather:

Snowmen at Night by Caralyn Buehner (Phyllis Fogelman, 2002)

The Tale of Jack Frost by David Melling (Barrons, 2003)

Extending the Poem

Jack Frost Paintings

Students will enjoy painting wintry window scenes that look like Jack Frost's glittering handiwork.

Materials

❁ tempera paints (white and blue)
❁ old newspapers
❁ 9- by 12-inch sheets of white construction paper
❁ paintbrushes
❁ iridescent glitter
❁ 12- by 16-inch sheets of brown construction paper
❁ 1- by 9-inch strips of brown paper (one per child)
❁ 1- by 12-inch strips of brown paper (one per child)
❁ small sequin snowflakes (found in craft stores)
❁ glue

1. Mix a small amount of blue paint into the white paint to create a very light blue color.

2. Cover the work surface with newspapers, then provide each child with a sheet of white construction paper. Have children use a paintbrush to cover their page with "frost"—the light blue paint.

3. Tell students to use the end of their paintbrush to scratch swirls and other designs into the "frost."

4. Children can then sprinkle glitter over the wet paint. Allow time to dry.

5. Have students glue their painted scenes onto sheets of brown paper. Help them glue the brown paper strips across their designs in a crisscross manner to form windowpanes.

6. If they wish, students can glue on sequin snowflakes as finishing touches to their frosty window scenes.

A Valentine, Just for You!

Gluing on the ribbons.

Gluing on the lace.

Shaking on the glitter.

I can't wait to see your face!

Drawing on the X's.

Drawing on the O's.

Writing words, "I love you

from my head down to my toes!"

Going down the hallway.

Heading to your room.

Carrying a valentine.

Dear _____,

just for you!

A Valentine, Just for You!

A Valentine, Just for You!

Introducing the Poem

🌀 Write the poem on chart paper. Draw a large heart around the words.

🌀 Before reading the poem aloud, fill in the generic name of a family member on the blank line (for example, *Mommy* or *Grandpa*). Later, students can personalize the poem.

🌀 Invite children to come up with ideas for acting out the poem. As you read each line, they may want to pretend to be spreading glue, shaking on glitter, drawing X's and O's, and so on.

Talking About the Poem

❀ Go around the circle and ask each child to name someone special they would like to make a valentine for. Write down their ideas on sticky notes. Reread the poem several more times, using the sticky notes to substitute a different name in the last line each time.

❀ Write each of the *-ing* words in the poem on a sticky note. (Make two notes for the words *gluing* and *drawing*, which appear twice in the poem.) Randomly pass out the notes. Have children take turns finding and covering the *-ing* word in the poem that matches the *-ing* word on their sticky note.

Working With Words

Valentine Rhyme Match-Up: Here's a simple matching game that children can play in honor of Valentine's Day. Photocopy the heart-shaped word cards on page 44 onto red construction paper. Photocopy the picture cards on page 45 onto white paper. Make several photocopies of both pages. Cut apart the picture cards and glue each one to the front of an envelope. Cut out the heart-shaped cards. Divide the class into small groups. Provide each group with a set of envelopes and a set of hearts. Review the words and pictures with students, then have group members work together to slip each heart into the envelope that shows the corresponding rhyming word. Bring the class back together again to check each group's matches. (To give children practice with different words, use correction fluid to mask the words on the hearts. Then program as desired.)

Shared Writing

Step-by-Step Directions: Many children are well-versed in the art of making valentines. Ask students to tell you what you need to make a valentine, such as paper, crayons, scissors, glitter, glue, markers, and so on. List their ideas. Then ask students to tell you step by step, how to make a valentine. Ask questions such as, "What do you do first? Then what do you do?" List the steps as students dictate them to you.

> ### How to Make a Valentine
> 1. Draw a heart on the paper.
> 2. Color the heart.
> 3. Cut out the heart.
> 4. Write a message.
> 5. Decorate the heart with ribbons, lace, and glitter.

Extending the Poem

Just-for-You Valentine Collages

Students personalize the poem "A Valentine, Just for You!" then use it as the centerpiece of a valentine collage for a loved one.

Materials

- poem (page 41)
- scissors
- 12- by 18-inch sheets of construction paper (red, pink, and purple)
- glue
- paper doilies
- stickers
- ribbon
- buttons
- scraps of lace or paper doilies
- scraps of paper (red, pink, and purple)
- glitter or glitter markers

1. Distribute photocopies of the poem to students. Have each child write the name of a loved one on the blank line. Then have each child color the heart and cut it out.

2. Let children choose a red, pink, or purple sheet of paper, onto which they can glue their personalized version of the poem.

3. Invite students to create a collage around the poem using the various art materials.

4. Have children sign their valentine collages before presenting them to loved ones.

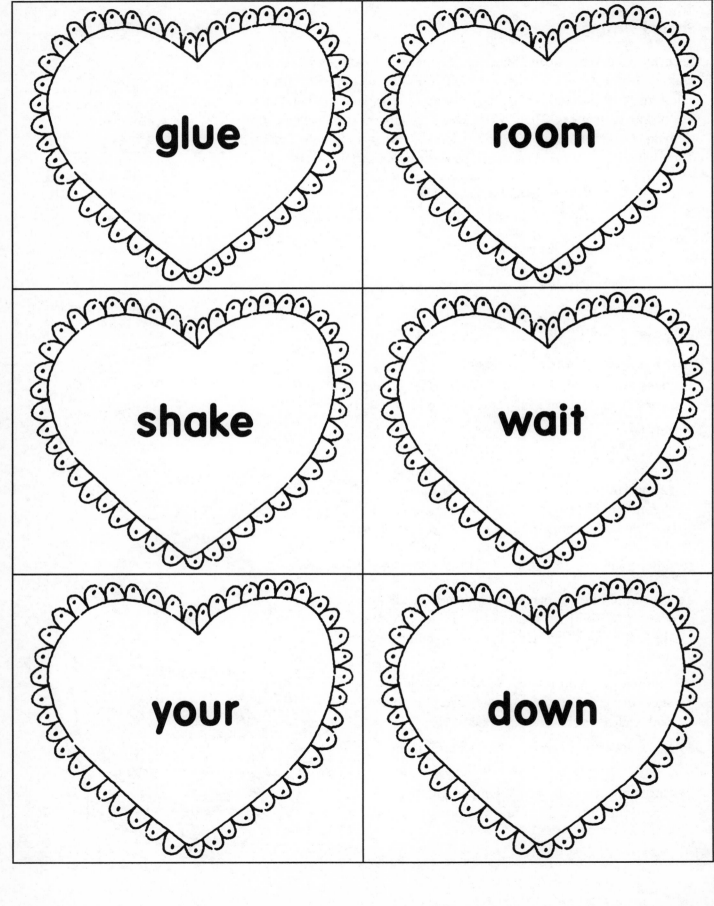

glue

room

shake

wait

your

down

Picture Cards

Springtime Magic

Roaring in like a lion,
bouncing out like a lamb,
spring is making magic
over all the land.
Pushing up the flowers,
painting on the leaves,
warming up the weather,
waking up the trees.
Bringing back the bluebirds,
spreading sunny cheer,
spring is making magic,
making winter disappear!

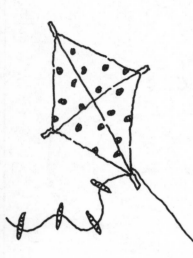

Circle-Time Poetry: Around the Year Scholastic Teaching Resources

Springtime Magic

Introducing the Poem

☉ Write the poem on chart paper. Draw the outline of a tulip around the words.

☉ Have children help you come up with sounds and hand gestures to accompany a reading of the poem. For example, they can roar after reading the first line to suggest spring coming in like a lion. They can "bounce" like a lamb, wave a make-believe magic wand, swish a pretend paintbrush, and so on, to act out other lines.

Talking About the Poem

❀ Ask students what it is about spring that seems magical to them. How do they feel when spring arrives? What do they see in nature or do on a spring day that makes them feel this way?

❀ Talk about the first two lines of the poem. Have students ever heard the expression, "March comes in like a lion and goes out like a lamb?" What do they think it means?

❀ Ask children to help you find and underline all the words that end in -ing.

❀ The letters *l, m, p, w, b,* and *s* are prominently featured in this poem. Invite children to help you hunt for and circle these letters at the beginning and endings of words.

Working With Words

Spring Things Match-Up: Cut pictures from magazines of "spring things" (for example, a flower, bird, kite, worm, rabbit). Glue these pictures to blank index cards. Write the corresponding word for each of the pictures on a separate index card. Mix up the cards and challenge students to match the picture cards with the word cards.

Shared Writing

Spring-y Sentences: Write the following sentence frame on the chalkboard several times:

Spring is ＿＿＿＿＿＿ ＿＿＿＿＿＿.

Ask children to name something they see or hear in the spring. Write this word on the second blank line. Then ask children to think of an *-ing* word that describes what this creature or thing does. Write the *-ing* word on the first blank line.

For example: Spring is <u>wiggling</u> <u>worms</u>.

(Continues)

Literature Links

Build students' enthusiasm for spring's arrival with these books, which all highlight the magical changes this season brings to the natural world:

Mud Makes Me Dance in the Spring by Charlotte Agell (Tilbury House, 1994)

The Springs of Joy by Tasha Tudor (Simon & Schuster, 1998)

Spring's Sprung by Lynn Plourde (Simon & Schuster, 2002)

Springtime by Ann Schweninger (Penguin, 1995)

Continue to model writing as children provide new phrases to complete the frame. Then give each child a copy of the tulip pattern on page 49. (Photocopy the page onto heavyweight paper for added durability.) Help students complete the sentence frame on the pattern. Have students then illustrate their sentence, fill in their name, and cut out the tulip. Punch holes along the left edges of the tulips and bind them together to make a class shape-book. Glue a green tagboard stem and leaves to the back of the book so that the stem extends below the flower.

Extending the Poem

Welcome Spring! Banner

Children will enjoy creating a bold, beautiful banner to welcome spring.

Materials

- ❀ sheet of white bulletin board paper (about 6 to 8 feet long)
- ❀ colored markers
- ❀ tempera paints (in bright spring colors)
- ❀ paintbrushes
- ❀ assorted magazines
- ❀ scissors
- ❀ glue

1. Write *Welcome Spring!* in bubble letters on the bulletin board paper. Make the letters as large as possible.

2. Invite children to paint each letter a different color.

3. Have children look through the magazines and cut out pictures that remind them of spring.

4. After the paint has dried on the banner, invite children to glue the pictures inside the letters, trimming the pictures as needed.

5. Display your banner on a wall. Use it to spark discussions that are centered around what students like best about spring.

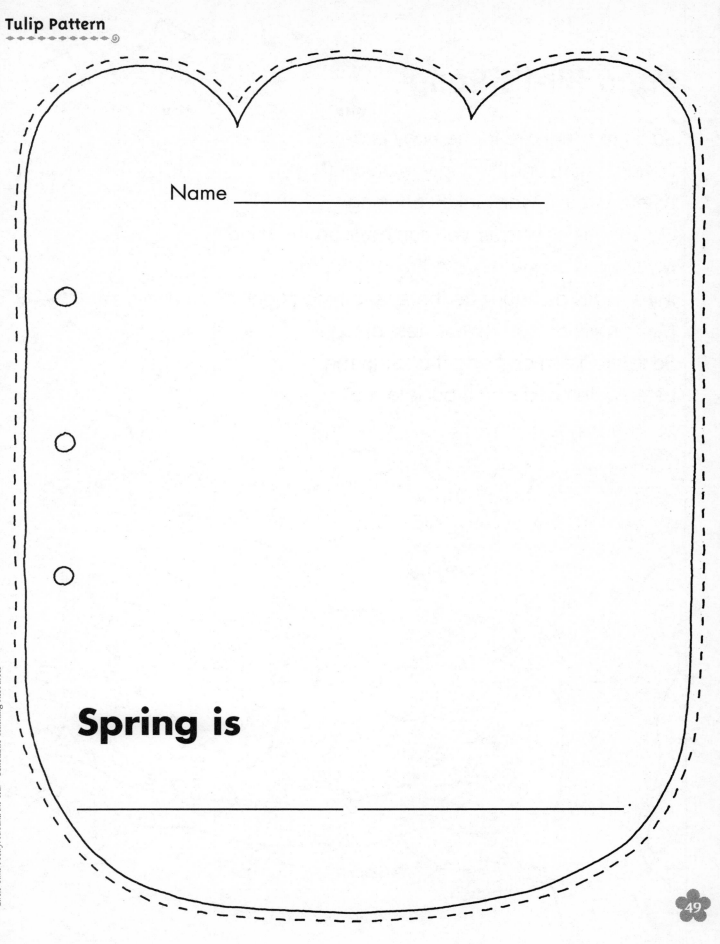

Name _____

Spring is

_____ _____.

Papa Bird's Song

Said the papa bird to the baby bird:

"Listen, listen, and I'll sing you a song.

Listen, listen, it won't take very long.

My song is a whisper you can hear on the wind.

My song is as sweet as a flower in spring.

My song is as happy as the sun shining bright.

My song is as soft as our nest at night.

So listen, listen and sing it back to me.

Listen, listen and sing it back to me."

Circle-Time Poetry: Around the Year Scholastic Teaching Resources

Papa Bird's Song

Introducing the Poem

@ Write the poem on chart paper. Draw a large oval around the text to represent the bird's body. Draw a small circle next to the large circle for the bird's head. Add an eye, beak, and wings—even musical notes if you like.

@ Read the poem using papa and baby bird puppets as props. (See "Extending the Poem," page 52, for directions.) Tell children you are going to be the papa bird and they are going to be baby birds who repeat what their papa says. Then as you read each line aloud, have children echo it back to you.

Talking About the Poem

✿ Ask children how they learn to do new things. How did they learn to brush their teeth, tie their shoes, and say the alphabet? Based on the poem, how do they think baby birds learn to sing? Tell students that young birds are like tape recorders: They listen to adult birds and repeat what they hear.

✿ Reread each line several times, emphasizing the many examples of alliteration. Pause after each line and ask children what sound or sounds they hear repeated. Invite volunteers to underline the letters that make these sounds.

Working With Words

Rhyming Words Chant: Play a rhyming game using the papa bird/baby bird echoing technique. Choose a pair of rhyming words from the poem such as *song* and *long*. In a sing-song voice say: "Song rhymes with long." Children then chant back: "Song rhymes with long." Come up with rhymes for other words in the poem (for example, *nest/best, sing/ring, me/key*) and continue playing the game. Once children get the hang of it, let them take turns being the "papa bird" leading the chant.

Shared Writing

Song Similes: Review with students the things that the papa bird compares his song to in the poem. Then write the following sentence frames on the chalkboard:

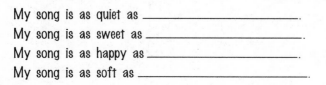

My song is as quiet as ⎯⎯⎯⎯⎯⎯⎯⎯⎯.
My song is as sweet as ⎯⎯⎯⎯⎯⎯⎯⎯⎯.
My song is as happy as ⎯⎯⎯⎯⎯⎯⎯⎯⎯.
My song is as soft as ⎯⎯⎯⎯⎯⎯⎯⎯⎯.

(Continues)

Learn more about birds and their songs by sharing these books with students:

Marsh Music by Marianne Berkes (Millbrook, 2003)

Robins: Songbirds of Spring by Mia Posada (Carolrhoda, 2004)

Songbirds: The Language of Song by Sylvia A. Johnson (Lerner, 2000)

The Song of Six Birds by Rene Deetlefs (Penguin Putnam, 1999)

Challenge students to think of new comparisons with which to complete the sentence frames. Ask questions to spark their thinking (for example, "What can you think of besides a whisper that is really quiet? What else is very soft?"). Encourage students to come up with several different ideas for completing each sentence.

Extending the Poem

Bird-Puppet Pattern Songs

Students make papa bird and baby bird puppets to use in make-believe singing lessons.

Materials

* bird puppet patterns (page 53)
* file folders (cut in half along the fold)
* glue
* scissors
* crayons
* craft sticks

❶ Provide each child with a copy of the pattern page and one half of a file folder.

❷ Have students glue the pattern page to the file folder.

❸ Children should then color and cut out the papa bird and baby bird patterns.

❹ To complete their puppets, show students how to glue each of their patterns to a craft stick.

❺ Students can use their puppets to pretend they are papa birds teaching baby birds to sing. Divide the class into pairs. Let one child in each pair be the adult bird. Have that child "sing" a simple pattern of tweets or chirps that the second child—the baby bird—will echo back. After trying a few "songs," have partners switch roles.

Celebrate the Earth

Celebrate the earth with me,
the oceans, meadows, mountains, trees.
I'll celebrate the earth with you,
the flowers, people, creatures, too.
Let's celebrate the earth together,
new green grass, exciting weather.
Celebrate the earth with me.
Let's share delight in all we see.

Circle-Time Poetry: Around the Year Scholastic Teaching Resources

Celebrate the Earth

Introducing the Poem

Celebrate the Earth

⚙ Use a blue marker to draw a large circle on a sheet of chart paper to represent the planet Earth. Use a green marker to write the poem inside the circle. If you wish, shade in a few land masses along the edges of the Earth so that they don't interfere with the text.

⚙ Show students a picture of Earth photographed from space. What do they think the blue parts are? What about the green and tan parts? (If there are clouds visible in the photo, ask students to guess what these areas are as well.)

⚙ Have children repeat each line of the poem after you read it aloud. You may want to stand in a circle holding hands to symbolize the theme of togetherness.

Talking About the Poem

✿ Begin a discussion about the beautiful and delightful planet we live on. Ask students to share with you some things about our wonderful world that they would like to celebrate.

✿ Reread the poem and have children raise their hands every time they hear the word *celebrate*. Point out the /s/ sound the letter *c* makes at the beginning of the word. Ask students what other sound the letter *c* makes. What other letter makes the /s/ sound?

✿ Invite a volunteer to underline all of the *m* words in the poem. What other *m* words do students know?

Working With Words

Geography Word Match-Up: Cut pictures from magazines that represent the geography-related words in the poem such as *oceans*, *meadows*, *mountains*, and *earth*. Find pictures for other terms as well, such as *valley*, *lake*, *river*, and *hill*. Paste these pictures to blank index cards. Write the corresponding word for each of the pictures on a separate card. Mix up the cards and challenge students to match the picture cards with the word cards.

Shared Writing

Write a Thank-You Note: What things about our planet are students thankful for? Why are they thankful for these things? Have students share their ideas as you model how to write a thank-you note to the Earth.

> Dear Earth,
> Thank you for the wild flowers.
> They are beautiful and cheer me up.
> Love,
> Sasha

Literature Links

Here are some wonderful books to encourage students to think about the delicate beauty of our planet and to remind them that we are all its caretakers:

Brother Eagle, Sister Sky: A Message from Chief Seattle by Susan Jeffers (Penguin, 1991)

Dear Children of the Earth: A Letter from Home by Schim Schimmel (Creative Publishing, 1994)

Earth Is Good: A Chant in Praise of Nature by Michael Demunn (Scholastic, 1999)

Extending the Poem

Paper Plate Planets

In this activity, children make paper-plate planets and write thank-you notes to Earth for sharing its gifts.

Materials

- old newspapers
- paper plates
- tempera paints (blue, green, and white)
- paintbrushes
- 12- by 18-inch sheets of white construction paper
- glue
- markers

1. Spread out newspapers and provide each child with a paper plate.

2. Have students paint their plate blue, green, and white. Students don't have to paint continents and oceans. They can simply swirl the paints together to create an impression of what the Earth looks like from space. Allow time for the paint to dry.

3. Have children glue their plate to a sheet of white paper. (The plate should be positioned on the paper so that there is space left below for writing, as shown.)

4. Help students write notes thanking the Earth for their favorite gifts in nature. Have students use the thank-you note you wrote in the Shared Writing activity (see page 55) as a model. Students can print their notes beneath the paper plates.

Dear Earth, Thank you for the trees. I like to look at them and climb them. Love, Ty

Mother Nature's Bouquet

Sweet joy! The flowers have come!
They've followed the showers.
They've grown with the sun.
They've risen up high.
They've spread their leaves.
They've opened their petals
to welcome the bees.
They've brightened the day
in their own sweet way.
They've grown to become
Mother Nature's bouquet!

Circle-Time Poetry: Around the Year Scholastic Teaching Resources

Mother Nature's Bouquet

Mother Nature's Bouquet

Introducing the Poem

🌀 Write the poem on chart paper. Draw a large circle around the words to represent the center of a flower. Draw petals around the circle.

🌀 Your class will enjoy acting out the poem as you read it aloud. Students can crouch down and pretend to be little flowers waiting to receive the showers and sunshine. Raise your hands high in the air and let your fingers "drizzle" down like rain. Hold your arms in a circle above your head to represent the sun coming out after the rain. The "flowers" can pretend to grow and bloom by slowly standing up and stretching out their arms.

Talking About the Poem

✿ Ask students if they have ever heard the saying, "April showers bring May flowers." What do they think it means? Begin a discussion about the things that plants need to grow.

✿ Circle the words *sweet, flowers, grown, from, green,* and *brightened.* Point out the consonant clusters at the beginnings of these words and model how to blend the sounds together.

✿ Place a sticky note under the words *sweet, bees,* and *green.* Say the words aloud several times. Ask students what sound these words have in common. Invite a volunteer to underline the double *ee* spelling pattern that makes the long-*e* sound in each word.

Working With Words

Initial Consonant Pass-Around: Bring in a beautiful spring flower and have children pass it around the circle. As each child receives the flower, he or she says a word beginning with the letter *f.* Repeat the game. This time, challenge children to remember and repeat all the preceding words before adding a new one as the flower moves around the circle. When the list of words gets too long to remember, start again.

Shared Writing

Flower List Poem: Write the word *Flowers* at the top of a sheet of chart paper. Ask children to think of words that describe flowers. List their ideas. Write the word *Flowers* again at the bottom of the list to conclude the poem.

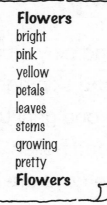

Flowers
bright
pink
yellow
petals
leaves
stems
growing
pretty
Flowers

Extending the Poem

May Bouquets

Your class can create its own beautiful May bouquet by making colorful flowers from coffee filters.

Materials

❀ old newspapers

❀ round coffee filters

❀ paper cups

❀ water

❀ food coloring (various colors)

❀ paintbrushes

❀ 12- by 18-inch sheets of light-green construction paper

❀ scraps of dark green construction paper

❀ scissors

❀ glue

❀ black markers

❁ **Literature Links** ❁

Here are several books that show how flowers add beauty to our world:

Miss Rumphius by Barbara Cooney (Penguin, 1985)

Planting a Rainbow by Lois Ehlert (Harcourt, 1992)

The Tiny Seed by Eric Carle (Simon & Schuster, 1991)

❶ Spread out newspapers and provide each child with two coffee filters stacked together. (Using two filters provides added durability.)

❷ Put about ¼ cup of water into each of a number of paper cups. Add 8 to 10 drops of food coloring to each cup. Set out enough cups for your class to share. Provide lots of different colors!

❸ Have children paint the colored water onto the filters. The filters will soak up the color beautifully to create delicate patterns. Allow time for for the filters to dry.

❹ Have children glue the "flower" onto a sheet of the light-green paper. (The flower should be positioned at the top of the sheet to leave room for a stem, as shown.) Children may want to twist or fold the coffee filters to create different-shaped flowers.

❺ Show students how to cut stems and leaves from the dark green paper. Then have them glue the stems and leaves onto their flowers.

❻ Children can copy your class list poem from the "Shared Writing" activity (see above) next to their flowers.

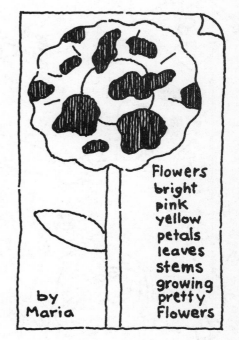

by Maria

Flowers
bright
pink
yellow
petals
leaves
stems
growing
pretty
Flowers

Run, Skip, Jump, and Play

Run and play! Run and Play!

Hop and skip right into May!

Laugh and grin! Laugh and grin!

Hum and holler! Twirl and spin!

For the days are warm and bright.

Skies are blue and the weather is right

to run and skip and hop and play,

to laugh and grin right into May!

Circle-Time Poetry: Around the Year Scholastic Teaching Resources

Run, Skip, Jump, and Play

Introducing the Poem

◉ Write the poem on chart paper. Draw a jump rope around the words.

◉ This poem has a strong rhythm. Invite children to clap to the beat as you read the poem aloud.

◉ Students may also enjoy moving to the poem. They can run, skip, and jump in place as you read the poem together.

Talking About the Poem

❂ Begin a discussion with children about all the fun games they can play outside when they run, jump, skip, and hop.

❂ This poem is full of playful action words. Invite students to help you find and circle all of them. They can then demonstrate each one. Challenge students to come up with other action words that describe what they do when they play (for example, *kick, catch, throw, hide*).

❂ Use sticky notes to cover the word *May* in lines 2 and 8, *spin* in line 4, and *right* in line 6. Reread the poem and ask children to try to guess the missing words. Provide guidance by pointing out the word each rhymes with.

Working With Words

Word Family Hop: Circle the word *hop* in the poem. Have children sound out each letter. Together, create a list of *-op* words such as *hop, pop, top, stop, flop, drop, bop, mop,* and *plop*. Invite children to hop as you read each word aloud. During recess or outside time, use chalk to write all the *-op* words on the sidewalk or playground. Have children take turns hopping from word to word. Lead the rest of the class in "hollering" each *-op* word as the child hopping lands on it.

Shared Writing

Springtime Play Comparison Chart: Begin a discussion about the different kinds of activities children might do outdoors on a sunny spring day and those they might do indoors on a rainy day. Talk about the noisy, energetic ways they play outdoors versus the quieter, less active ways they play indoors. Create a chart comparing their ideas.

Outside Activities	Inside Activities
running	reading
jumping	coloring
skipping	playing board games
playing ball	watching TV
riding bikes	playing cards

Literature Links

These fun-loving books show good friends sharing good times and celebrate the importance of play:

Hippopotamus, My Friend by Ruth Scheer, (Scheer Delight Publishing, 1999)

Jump Rope Magic by Afi-Odelia Scruggs (Scholastic, 2002)

Roxaboxen by Alice McLerran (HarperCollins, 1991)

Extending the Poem

Springtime Wind-Catchers

Have children make wind-catchers to run, skip, jump, and play with on the next sunny spring day.

Materials

✿ old newspapers
✿ paper plates
✿ tempera paints
✿ paintbrushes
✿ black markers
✿ crepe paper streamers (various colors)
✿ scissors
✿ glue

1 Spread out newspapers and provide each child with a paper plate. Have children paint both sides of their plate and allow to dry.

2 Invite children to use a marker to draw a happy face on one side of the plate to represent the joy of spring.

3 Have children cut different lengths of streamers. On the back of the plate, have them glue the streamers along one of the edges.

4 When the glue has dried, invite children to take their wind-catchers outside. They can watch the ribbons or streamers fly as they run, dance, and play.

Songs of Summer

Crickets begin their magical tune.
Ladybugs jig for the joy of June.
Dragonflies dance as they dart by.
Their whirring wings sing a lullaby.
Bumblebees buzz a melody sweet.
Caterpillars tap their many feet.
Oh, happy hearts beat just like drummers
as June brings on the songs of summer.

Circle-Time Poetry: Around the Year Scholastic Teaching Resources

Songs of Summer

Introducing the Poem

⊚ Write the poem on chart paper. Draw a few simple bugs around the poem, such as a dragonfly, ladybug, and bee.

⊚ As you read the poem aloud, have children move to the rhythm of the words. They can pretend they are ladybugs "jigging for joy," dragonflies flapping their wings, or caterpillars tapping their feet to the beat. Invite students to try a different movement each time you read the poem.

Talking About the Poem

✿ Ask children why they think the bugs in the poem are singing and dancing. Are students as happy as these bugs that summer has arrived? Why or why not?

✿ Reread each line several times, emphasizing the many examples of alliteration. Pause after each line and ask children what sound or sounds they hear repeated. Invite volunteers to underline the letters that makes these sounds.

Working With Words

Initial Consonant "Buzz": Children can pretend to be bumblebees as they play a game of "buzz" focusing on initial consonant sounds. Pick a consonant sound that is highlighted in the poem, such as /j/. Explain that you are going to say a list of words beginning with /j/. When students hear you say a word that doesn't begin with this sound, they should buzz like bees. For example: *June, joy, jig, jelly, joke, jack, blue . . . BZZZZZZZZ!* Continue playing the game using other initial consonant sounds featured in the poem such as /d/, /w/, /b/, /h/, and /s/ or consonant clusters such as /cr/, /dr/, /sw/, and /br/.

Shared Writing

All About Bugs Chart: Make a simple five-column chart on chart paper. At the top of each column, write the name of a bug mentioned in the poem. Under each heading, list all the things students know about that particular bug. Ask students to think about what the bug looks like, the sound it makes (if any), how it moves, where it lives, and so on. Keep the chart posted so you can add to it as students learn more about bugs.

Crickets	Ladybugs	Dragonflies	Bumblebees	Caterpillars
black	red with black	long	yellow and	green eat leaves
jump	spots	blue	black stripes	change into
noisy	small	shiny	fuzzy	butterflies
chirp	round	clear wings	buzz	
			sting	

Extending the Poem

Fingerprint Bugs!

Students will have fun turning their own fingerprints into whimsical bug bands.

Materials

❀ books and nature magazines (such as *Ranger Rick, My Big Backyard,* and *Owl*) that contain pictures of insects and spiders

❀ washable inkpads (various colors)

❀ white paper

❀ black felt tip pens

① Display the pictures of insects and spiders. Ask students to share their observations about the differences and similarities in the bugs' appearances. What do they notice about the shapes of the bugs' bodies? Which ones have wings? What other details do they notice?

② Demonstrate how to make fingerprint bugs using the inkpads. Model how to press fingertips onto the inkpads then onto the paper to make prints. Use a felt tip pen to add legs, heads, antennae, and other details.

③ Invite students to create their own fingerprint bugs. Can they make dragonflies? How about caterpillars and butterflies? Ladybugs? Spiders? Encourage students to use their imaginations as they experiment.

④ Show students how to add a few simple instruments (for example, guitars, horns, tambourines), to create a mini bug band.

Literature Links

These "buggy" books will introduce your students to a variety of insects and spiders and their fascinating characteristics:

Fireflies! by Julie Brikloe (Simon & Schuster, 1996)

Simon & Schuster's Children's Guide to Insects and Spiders by Jinny Johnson (Simon & Schuster, 1997)

The Very Clumsy Click Beetle by Eric Carle (Penguin Putnam, 1999)

The Very Quiet Cricket by Eric Carle (Penguin Putnam, 1997)

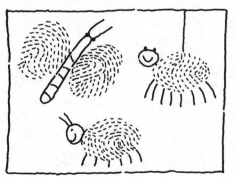

Lemonade in the Shade

When the sun is bright and hot
I like to find a leafy spot
and cool off in the shade.

It's nicer here among the trees
where I can feel the summer breeze
and sip my lemonade.

Circle-Time Poetry: Around the Year   Scholastic Teaching Resources

Lemonade in the Shade

Introducing the Poem

Lemonade in the Shade

⊚ Write the poem at the top of a sheet of chart paper. Draw the leafy outline of a treetop around the words. Add a tree trunk.

⊚ Have children come up with different actions to accompany each line of the poem. For example, they can wipe their brow to suggest the hot sun, put their hands up to their forehead to scout a leafy spot, fan themselves to suggest cooling off, and so on.

Talking About the Poem

✿ Will students be sipping "lemonade in the shade" this summer? Begin a discussion about how they plan to enjoy the summer season.

✿ Provide each of three volunteers with a different colored marker. Each volunteer can underline one of the three pairs of rhyming words in the poem, so that each pair is underlined in a different color. Ask students to look closely at the spelling patterns in each pair of rhyming words. Which rhyming words have the same spelling patterns? Which rhyming words have different spelling patterns?

✿ Invite children to find all the words in the poem beginning or ending with the letter *l*. Ask what sound this letter makes.

Working With Words

Initial Consonant Lemon Toss: Bring a lemon into class and have children pass it around the circle. As each child receives the lemon, he or she says a word beginning with the letter *l*. Repeat the game. This time, when children receive the lemon, they can try to remember and repeat all the preceding words before adding a new one. When the list of words gets too long to remember, start again.

Shared Writing

"Keep Cool!" Word Web: Sipping lemonade is a sweet way to cool off on a summer day. Ask children to think of other ways to keep cool when the weather is hot. Create a word web to show their ideas.

Here are several books that capture the joy of sunshiny summer days:

The First Sunbeam of Summer by Louise S. Phillips (Windswept House, 1996)

Summer by Alice Low (Random House, 2001)

Summer Sun Risin' by W. Nickola-Lisa (Lee & Low, 2002)

Wild, Wild, Sunflower Child by Nancy White Carlstrom (Simon & Schuster, 1991)

SAFETY NOTE:
Remind children never to look directly at the sun because it can harm their eyes.

Extending the Poem

Sunny Paint Cubes

Here's a great way to beat the summer heat: paint bright suns using tinted ice cubes.

Materials

✿ water
✿ tempera paint (orange and yellow)
✿ ice cube trays
✿ craft sticks
✿ 9- by 12-inch sheets of white construction paper

❶ Add water to the orange and yellow tempera paints. Thin the paints just enough to pour them easily into ice cube trays. Be careful not to add too much water or the paint colors will look washed out later.

❷ Place the paints in the freezer. When they are partially frozen, insert the craft sticks. Continue freezing until the paint cubes are solid.

❸ On the next hot day, take the class outside. Show children how to hold the ice cubes by the craft sticks and use them to paint on the white paper.

❹ Have children use the colored cubes to paint pictures of bright summer suns. Ask them how they think the real sun is helping them paint their pictures. Check that children understand that the sun's heat is actually melting the frozen paint cubes, turning them into a liquid again.

Summer Toes

One, two, three, four, five little toes.
Wiggly-giggly-barefoot-toes.
Piping-hot-sidewalk-toes.
Tickly-prickly-green-grass-toes.
Splishy-splashy-wet-wave-toes.
Scritchy-scratchy-sand-in-toes.
One, two, three, four, five little toes.

Circle-Time Poetry: Around the Year Scholastic Teaching Resources

Summer Toes

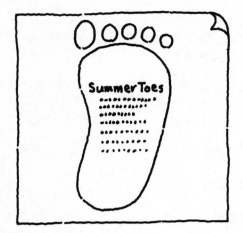

Introducing the Poem

◎ Write the poem on chart paper. Draw the outline of a foot around the words. Don't forget to include five cute little toes!

◎ Before reading the poem, have children take off their shoes and socks. Model how to use fingers to wiggle each toe on one foot while counting to five. When you read the first two lines of the poem, children should count their toes. They can wiggle all ten toes freely as you read lines 2 through 6.

Talking About the Poem

❀ Begin a discussion with children about how nice bare feet feel in the summer. Reread lines 2 through 6 of the poem. Pause after each line and ask children to describe where the bare toes are and what they are doing. Ask students to imagine that their own bare toes are stepping on the sidewalk, in the water, over the sand, and through the grass. Ask them to show you how they would walk over each surface and to describe what it might feel like.

❀ Ask students what letter the word *toes* begins with, then invite them to count how many times the word *toes* appears in the poem. Can they find two other words that begin with *t*?

Working With Words

Initial Consonant Tiptoe: Write the word *tiptoe* on chart paper and have a volunteer circle the *t*'s. Then invite children to tiptoe around in a circle as you recite a list of words beginning with the letter *t*. When they hear you say a word that doesn't begin with *t*, students should immediately stop tiptoeing. Students can resume tiptoeing when you begin to recite *t* words again.

Shared Writing

Summertime Sentence Foot Book: What will students' toes be doing this summer? Provide each child with a copy of the footprint pattern on page 72. (Photocopy the page onto heavyweight paper for added durability.) On chart paper, copy the sentence frame that appears on the pattern and model how to complete it. Then help each student complete the sentence on his or her pattern. Students can then illustrate their sentence, fill in their name, and cut out the pattern. Punch holes along the left edges of the patterns and bind them together to make a class shape-book.

Extending the Poem

Footprint Butterflies

Here's a fun way to celebrate bare summer feet: Make footprint butterflies!

Materials

❀ old newspapers

❀ washable paints (various colors)

❀ paintbrushes

❀ 9- by 12-inch sheets of white construction paper

❀ paper towels

❀ black markers

❀ several shallow pans of warm, soapy water

❶ Spread newspapers over your work surface. Have children take off their shoes and socks.

❷ Allow each child to choose what color he or she would like to make his or her butterfly. Have children take turns sitting in a chair as you use a paintbrush to apply paint to their bare feet.

❸ Slide a sheet of white paper beneath each child's painted feet. The child should then put his or her feet down on the paper to make a pair of footprints. Check that children place their feet side by side on the paper, on a slight angle, leaving a few inches between them. The footprints will be the butterfly's wings.

❹ Help each child wash and dry his or her feet before moving on to make the next student's prints.

❺ After the paint has dried, have students use the black markers to draw their butterfly's body between the footprint wings. Then have them add antennae. Invite children to paint details on the wings, if they like.

✎ ◇ **Literature Links** ◇ ✐

Feet have all kinds of fun in these playful books:

Busy Toes by C.W. Bowie (Charlesbridge, 2002)

The Foot Book by Dr. Seuss (Random House, 1968)

Hello Toes! Hello Feet! by Ann Whitford Paul (DK Ink, 1998)

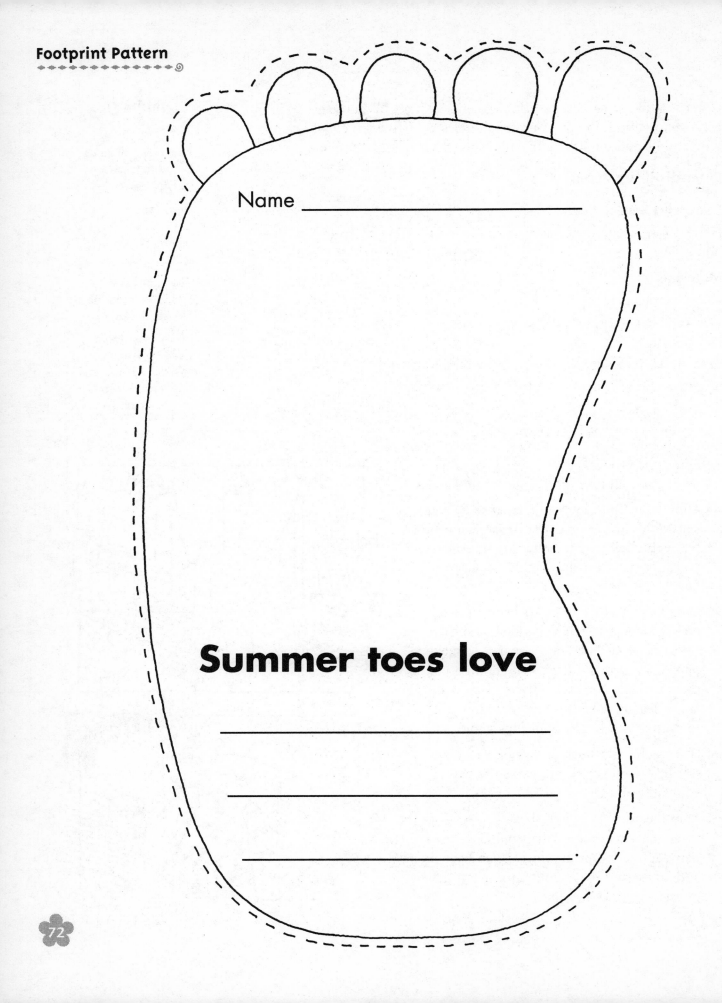

Name _____

Summer toes love

_____

_____

_____.

Circle-Time Poetry: Around the Year Scholastic Teaching Resources

Firecracker-Loud

Firecracker-loud
comes hot July.
Fireworks burst
across the sky.
Red, white, and blue
parade on by.
Hands clap, feet stomp,
drums bang, flags fly.
We celebrate!
We jump up high.
"Happy Birthday,
America!"
we all cry.

Circle-Time Poetry: Around the Year   Scholastic Teaching Resources

Firecracker-Loud

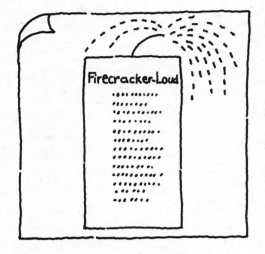

Introducing the Poem

🌀 Write the poem on chart paper. Draw the outline of a sparking firecracker around the poem.

🌀 Have children pretend that they are in a parade as you read the poem aloud. They can clap and march in place to the beat of the words. Invite children to jump as high as they can as you read line 10. As you read lines 11 and 12, they should shout "Happy Birthday, America!".

Talking About the Poem

✿ Begin a discussion about the Fourth of July. Do children know why this day is important? If children aren't sure, tell them it is America's birthday. Ask them to describe the different ways we celebrate this special day.

✿ Reread the first four lines of the poem. Then ask children if they have ever seen a fireworks display, outdoors or on television. Invite them to describe their memories and impressions.

✿ Use sticky notes to cover all the rhyming words in the poem: *July, sky, by, fly, high,* and *cry.* Challenge students to guess the missing words as you reread the poem. Offer guidance by telling them that all the missing words rhyme with *pie.*

✿ Place a sticky note under the words *loud, hot,* and *high.* Ask children to come up with opposites for these words.

Working With Words

Action Word Parade: Generate a list of noisy action words associated with parades (for example, *clapping, stomping, singing, drumming, tooting, yelling, laughing, cheering, banging, booming*). Write each word on each of two unlined index cards. (You'll need to use some words more than once.) Provide each child with a word card. Place the matching word cards faceup in the center of the circle. Have children find the word that matches the one on their cards. Invite children to parade around the room holding their word cards, imitating the sound that each card names.

Shared Writing

Five Senses Word Web: Parades give all of our senses a workout. In addition to the sounds they might hear, what might children see, smell, and taste at a parade? Create a word web to present their ideas.

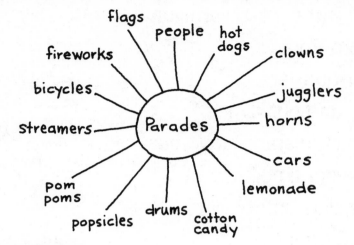

Literature Links

These books feature parades and fireworks displays to fuel students' enthusiasm for July 4th festivities:

Best Bug Parade by Stuart J. Murphy (HarperCollins, 1999)

Fourth of July Mice by Bethany Roberts (Clarion, 2004)

Hats Off for the Fourth of July by Harriet Ziefert (Penguin Putnam, 2002)

Parade by Donald Crews (HarperCollins, 1987)

Extending the Poem

Festive Fireworks

Students can create dazzling displays of festive fireworks in honor of the Fourth of July.

Materials

❖ pictures of fireworks displays (see Literature Links, right)
❖ 9- by 12-inch sheets of black construction paper
❖ glitter or glitter pens (various colors)
❖ glue
❖ bulletin board paper (in any bright color)
❖ black marker

❶ Share some of the pictures of fireworks with students. What do they notice about the colors and patterns? Leave the books on display as children create their own artwork.

❷ Demonstrate for children how to use the glitter pens or glitter and glue to create designs that look like fireworks (on the black paper). Then distribute black paper and other decorating materials to students and encourage them to experiment with making showers, bursts, swirls, and other designs as they create their own glittering pictures.

❸ Cover a bulletin board with the colored paper. Write the poem "Firecracker-Loud" at the center of the bulletin board and surround it with children's artwork.

Ice-Cream Evenings

When we hear a melody
calling from the street,
we know it is the ice-cream van
bringing us a treat.
Jingling our quarters,
our nickels, and our dimes,
we dash to choose our favorites
each and every time.
Sweet licks slide smoothly
down our throats
in the most delightful way.
Creamy, dreamy ice-cream evenings
melt the heat away.

Circle-Time Poetry: Around the Year   Scholastic Teaching Resources

Ice-Cream Evenings

Introducing the Poem

◎ Draw the outline of a double scoop of ice cream on a sheet of chart paper. Add an ice-cream cone beneath it. Write the text of the poem inside the ice cream.

◎ Have children act out the poem as you read it aloud. For example, they can cup hands to their ears to pretend they are listening for the ice-cream truck, jingle imaginary coins in their hands, run in place as they dash for the van, lick make-believe ice-cream cones, and rub their tummies.

Talking About the Poem

✿ Begin a discussion with children about the different kinds of treats they can get from the ice-cream truck (or the store). Which are their favorites?

✿ Use the poem to focus on short *i*- and long *i*-sounds. Invite volunteers to circle all the words in the poem that have *i* in them. Say each word aloud several times and ask children whether they hear the long- or short-*i* sound.

Working With Words

Vowel Ice-Cream Cones: Continue working with long- and short *i*-sounds. Make four copies of page 79. Cut out the scoops of ice cream and write either a short-*i* or long-*i* word on each of them. (See lists, right.) From light brown construction paper, cut out two cone shapes. Write *long i* on one cone, and *short i* on the other. Tape the cones, side by side, to a sheet of chart paper. Read to children the *long-i* and *short-i* labels that are printed on the cones. Then pronounce the sounds that correspond to the labels. Next, read the word on each ice-cream scoop, drawing out the long- or short-*i* sound. Ask children whether they hear long *i* or short *i*, then invite them to tape the scoop on top of the cone with the corresponding label. Continue building multi-decker ice-cream cones until you've sorted all the word cards.

Short-i words
big
did
fish
fix
hit
it
pig
six

long-i words
bike
dime
five
ice
kite
like
mice
shine

Literature Links

Children will "eat up" these stories which are about ice-cream treats and the people who serve them:

The Good Humor Man by Kathleen N. Daly (Golden Books, 2001)

Isaac the Ice Cream Truck by Scott Santoro (Henry Holt, 1999)

Shared Writing

Ice-Cream List Poem: This is a fun verse to use as a springboard for creating a list poem. Children are sure to come up with wonderful ways to describe ice cream, its colors and flavors, and the way it feels sliding down their throats. List the words they use on a piece of chart paper. Begin and end the poem with the words *Ice Cream*.

Ice Cream
cold
creamy
scoops
smooth
sweet
chocolate
strawberry
delicious
Ice Cream

Extending the Poem

Ice-Cream Cone Mobiles

Cool off your classroom with these multicolored ice-cream cone mobiles.

✿ ice-cream cone pattern (page 80)
✿ crayons
✿ black markers
✿ scissors
✿ hole punch
✿ yarn (in ice-cream colors, such as pink, brown, and light green)
✿ coat hangers

1 Provide each child with a copy of the ice cream cone pattern. Tell children to write their name and favorite ice-cream flavor on the lines provided.

2 Invite children to color their ice-cream to match their favorite flavor. Then have children cut out their cone. They may want to draw chocolate chips, nuts, or other "extras" onto their ice cream, and color the cone.

3 Have children write two or three words that describe ice cream on the back of their ice-cream scoop. Then have them color this side of the pattern as well. You may want to keep your list poem from the "Shared Writing" activity (see above) on display to help children choose and spell words.

4 Punch a hole in the top of each ice-cream cone pattern.

5 Cut different lengths of yarn. Loop a piece of yarn through the hole at the top of each pattern. Tie the yarn to the coat hangers to create mobiles. Display the mobiles around your classroom.

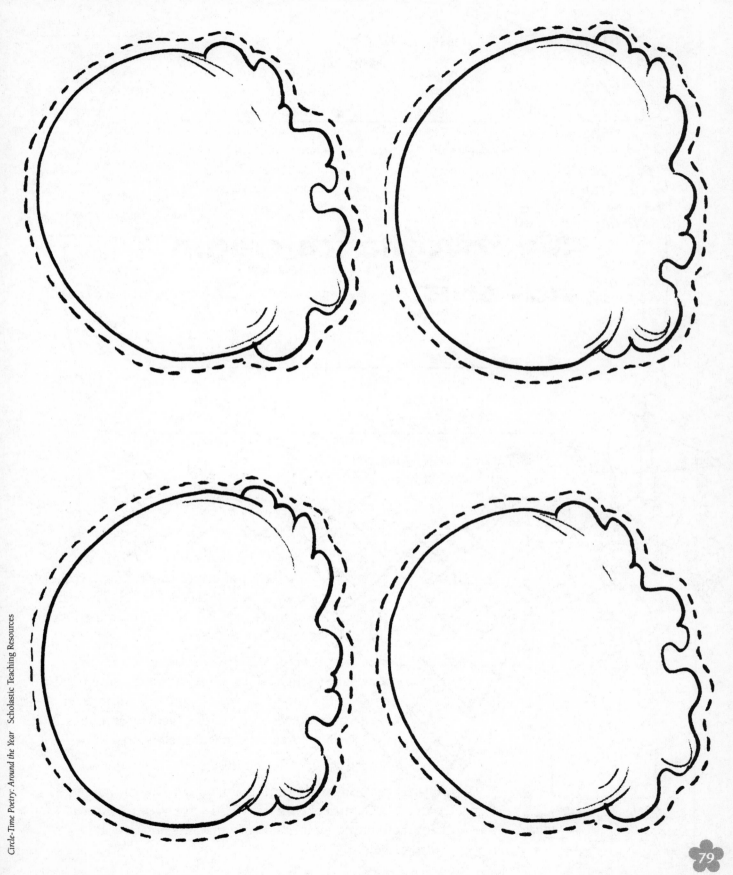

Name _____

My favorite ice-cream flavor is

_____

_____.

Circle-Time Poetry: Around the Year   Scholastic Teaching Resources